Amina's Bracelets

A Kidpreneur Story

By Tasha Danielle, CPA
Illustrations By Hikari

Copyright © 2016 by Financial Garden LLC. All right reserved.
Published in the United States by Financial Garden LLC.
No part of this book may be reproduced in any format, without written permission of the publisher.

For Mary Lee Long with love
and
In memory of Clementine Thomas Nobles

Amina and her mom went to the store. While in the store, Amina saw the brand-new tablet that all her friends were talking about at school. She grabbed the tablet and ran over to her mom and exclaimed,

"Mommy, this is the brand-new tablet that all my friends are getting! Can you please buy this for me? It's only $160.00!"

"Amina, you're only nine years old. I'm not spending $160.00 on something that you are probably going to lose or break," said Amina's mom.

"Mommy, PLEASE!" Amina shrieked.

"If you want this tablet, you will have to spend your own money," said Amina's mom.

While walking to the car with her mom, Amina thought to herself, "I don't have $160.00 – I only earn $10.00 a week doing chores." Amina realized that she would have to just wait until her birthday or even all the way until Christmas to get the tablet. To Amina, both her birthday and Christmas seemed so far away.

Amina was still sad when she and her mom got home. Amina went to the kitchen to talk to her big brother Justin.

"What's wrong Amina?" asked Justin.

"I really want the new tablet that all of my friends have, but Mommy told me that I would have to buy it with my own money," Amina said.

"Haven't you been saving money from doing your chores?" Justin asked.

"Yes, but I only have $30.00 in my piggy bank. I'll never be able to save $160.00," said Amina.

"Well, you only need $130.00 more to buy the tablet. If you saved your entire $10.00 allowance for the next 13 weeks, you will be able to buy the tablet," Justin said.

"How far away is 13 weeks?" Amina asked.

"It's the end of February now, so by the first week of June you will be able to buy the new tablet!" said Justin.

"I won't be able to play new video games or video chat with my friends until the end of the school year?" said Amina disappointedly.

Amina walked to the living room to see if she could convince her dad to buy the tablet.

"Daddy, I really want a new tablet. Mommy said that I would have to buy the tablet with my money. But I only have $30.00 saved in my piggy bank. I won't have enough money to buy the tablet until June," Amina said.

"Yes, I understand that it will take a long while to save that kind of money, but there is another way you can earn the money," said her dad.

"You can become an entrepreneur!" said Amina's dad excitedly. Amina tried to say "entrepreneur" and had a little trouble.

"What's an entreee…?" she asked.

"Say it with me, entrepreneur," said her dad.

Amina's dad explained to her that an entrepreneur is a person who starts their own business to earn money. Amina's dad also told her that kids could start their own business! Amina got excited and named a business that she could start.

"Oh, like a lemonade stand?" Amina said.

"Yes, that's one example, but that's not the only way a kid can start a business. The best way an entrepreneur starts their business is by doing something they are talented in," explained Amina's dad.

"What is one of your talents?" Amina's dad asked as he stared at her wrist.

"I love making bracelets," she said.

"Exactly," said her dad with a smile. He then explained that the next step to starting a business was to find out if there was a "demand" for what the business is trying to sell. "Do you think there is a demand for your bracelets?" Amina's dad asked.

Amina had a puzzled look on her face. "A "demand"? I don't understand, Dad," she said.

"Demand means that there are people who are willing to pay money for your bracelets," said Amina's dad.

Amina's mom walked into the living room as Amina and her dad were talking.

"I know plenty of people who would buy Amina's bracelets. My co-workers ask me all the time where I purchased my bracelet. Are you thinking of selling your bracelets?" asked Amina's mom.

Amina had never thought about becoming an entrepreneur. But she could possibly get the new tablet faster by starting her own business. Amina and her mom discussed the risks involved with starting a business. One risk is that entrepreneurs don't always start off making a profit.

"You will have to make sure you set the price of your bracelets to cover the cost of the materials that you use to make the bracelets," explained Amina's mom.

Amina began to think about how much she had spent in the past for bracelet materials.

"Well, I can purchase the bands for $1.00 each, the charms and beads cost about $2.00 for each band," said Amina. "Okay, so it costs $3.00 to make a bracelet," said Amina's mom.

Amina and her mom determined that the selling price of each bracelet would be $7.50. Amina would make a profit of $4.50 for each bracelet she sold.

"Can I spend the $30.00 in my piggy bank to buy materials for 10 bracelets?" asked Amina.

"I know that we usually make you keep at least $10.00 in your piggy bank, but this time we will allow you to spend all of your savings," said her mom.

Amina and her mom went to the craft store to buy materials for the bracelets. After leaving the craft store and returning home, they spent the afternoon making bracelets.

The next day, Amina went to her mom's job and sold all 10 bracelets, making $75.00! Amina and her mom were overjoyed about the sale of the bracelets!

Amina and her mom went back to the craft store to buy more bracelet materials. As they walked in, Amina saw a flyer for a craft show coming to town. Amina pointed out the flyer to her mom.

"I think this would be a great way to sell your bracelets! If you want to do this, I will help you make more bracelets," said Amina's mom.

"Great! Thanks Mom! I have enough money to buy materials for 25 bracelets to sell at the craft show!" exclaimed Amina.

Over the next couple of weeks, Amina and her mom made the bracelets for the upcoming craft show.

It was finally showtime! Amina couldn't wait to sell her bracelets. Amina's parents were at the craft show to help her sell her bracelets.

Amina became a bit nervous when talking to potential customers. However, Amina sold all 25 bracelets, earning a total of $187.50! Amina now had enough money to buy the tablet and to put $27.50 back into her piggy bank!

Amina and her parents went to the store to purchase the tablet.

"I know I bought my tablet, but I want to keep selling my bracelets!" said Amina.

"We're so proud of you Amina! We will help you create a budget to make sure you have a successful business!" said her parents.

About the Author

Tasha Danielle, CPA, is an advocate for youth financial literacy. She founded Financial Garden LLC (financialgarden.net) to financially empower students of all ages. Amina's Bracelets is Tasha's first published book. Tasha resides in Metro Detroit.

About the Illustrator

Derrick Stewart II is a graphic designer and illustrator out of the Detroit area. Inspired by Japanese language and culture, Derrick chose the name Hikari for his brand. Derrick enjoys bringing creative solutions through his designs and illustrations. Find him on Instagram here: @tenchihikari.

www.ingramcontent.com/pod-product-compliance
Lightning Source LLC
LaVergne TN
LVHW072103070426
835508LV00002B/241